I am a child

A cry for the rights of creativity and childhood in education

I AM A CHILD

The first five or six years of my life are the most precious of my lifetime.

They cannot be repeated.

They cannot be redeemed or recaptured.

If they are wasted then they are lost forever.

In life...

"THE WINTER IS LONG

THE AUTUMN IS LONG

THE SUMMER IS LONG

BUT THE SPRING IS SO SHORT"

Parents and teachers – you have my springtime in your hands.

You can make it wonderful or you can destroy it.

The pressures and demands of Ofsted try to take my childhood away from me.

I do not want tests and curriculums, measurements and targets.

My childhood doesn't need them. I am only beginning my life.

Please let me **be a child** for six years.

I hope that by reading this book you will help to save my childhood

FOR MY SPRING IS SO SHORT

Please don't let them take it away from me.

TAPSTEP

Roger's Daddy's clever,

Daisy's flies a plane,

Michael's does computers

and has a house in Spain.

Lucy's goes to London,

he stays there every week ...

　　But my Daddy has an ear-ring

　　　and lovely dancing feet.

He hasn't got a brief case,

he hasn't got a phone,

he hasn't got mortgage

and we haven't got a home.

He hasn't got a fax machine,

we haven't got a car.

　　But he can dance and fiddle

　　　and my Daddy is

　　　　a Star.

A poem written after watching a small child begging with her Dad.

However kind or unkind, rich or poor, efficient or inept we are as teachers or parents, our children trust us and follow us. They are utterly faithful and believing. (Not so their adolescent brothers and sisters!) It is very easy to exploit young children's trust, for they always try to do whatever we ask...

Politicians, via the National Curriculum, SATS and Literacy Hour, have exploited children in their crazed attempt to score political advantage via Ofsted reports, scores, tests and league tables. Headteachers have grudgingly gone along with it.

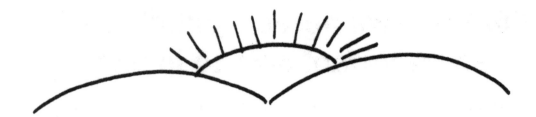

I AM IN THE BEST SCHOOL

I'm in the best school,
I'm in the learning class,
I'm learning every morning,
I'm learning really fast.

I have a desk and folder,
I can write my name,
I'm doing rather nicely
and my lessons have an aim.

I can say my letters,
do numbers one to ten,
I can hold a pencil
and I can hold a pen.

My teacher gives me homework,
my sister gets it too.
People say I'm gifted
so I think it must be true.

They've put me in the fast track
and I hope I'll be OK –
I learnt to read quite quickly
but I never learnt to play.

Oh Yes – we agree – childhood is so important and so is play!

SO TRUE SAY PARENTS AND TEACHERS

We couldn't agree with you more!

Peter Dixon says:

As an educational consultant, ex-early years teacher and lately senior lecturer in education (and Southampton supporter and children's writer), I question whether we really do believe in childhood. Many Ofsted inspectors who go round planning and implementing wrongful ideas don't seem to!

Unfortunately numerous parents and teachers seem willing to accept the inappropriate work seen in many of our schools. They tend to believe whatever Ofsted and newspapers tell them.

INAPPROPRIATE WORK RUINS CHILDHOOD

Charles Kingsley saw the same problem 150 years ago.

From *Water Babies*
by Charles Kingsley

"You see," said the stick, "there were as pretty little children as you could wish to see, and might have been so still if they had been only left to grow up like human beings, and then handed over to me; but their foolish fathers and mothers, instead of letting them pick flowers, and make dirt pies and get birds' nests, and dance around the gooseberry bush, as little children should, kept them always at lessons, working, working, working, learning weekday lessons all weekdays, and Sunday lessons all Sunday, and weekly examinations every Saturday, and monthly examinations every month, and yearly examinations every year, everything seven times over, as if once was not enough, and enough as good as a feast – till their brains grew big, and their bodies grew small, and they were all changed into turnips, with little but water inside; and still their foolish parents actually pick the leaves off them as fast as they grow, lest they should have anything green about them."

Since the advent of Ofsted, too much education seems to have slumped into the condition Charles Kingsley observed 150 years ago.

And although a few brave educationalists and forward thinking county and city councils attempt to relight the lamp of childhood – it is a struggle. The overall scene is one of children being manipulated to meet the requirements of politicians, Ofsted and Headteachers. This way they can boast of supposedly higher standards. But it is all at the children's expense.

Parents are often tricked into believing that test scores, league tables and even 'boosting' children is the hallmark of a good school.

It certainly isn't the case. All too often children are 'trained' to do well at tests, losing the real experience and joys of childhood and learning in the process.

BOOSTER PRIMARY

I am a 'booster boy',
I'm in the booster class,
I'm boosted every morning,
I'm boosted really fast ...

I have a booster teacher,
we do our booster tests.
Booster on my jacket,
booster on my vest.

Yes, I am a booster boy,
I get to school at dawn
for extra special boosting
in the special booster form.

I do not mind being boosted –
people say it's right –
so I boost away in daytime
and I wet the bed all night.

Did you know?

Between the ages of 3 and 5 every child must be 'measured' to one of the nine levels in each of 13 areas.

"Personal, social and emotional communication, language and literacy, mathematical knowledge and understanding of the world", and so on...

That is, – "in a class of 30, there are **390** boxes to be ticked from a finely graded choice of **3510**. At the end of foundation stage every five year old is to be marked (labelled) out of 117." (John Clare)

circa. 2002

HOW ON EARTH HAVE TEACHERS AND PARENTS COME TO ACCEPT THIS?

WHY DO THEY MOAN AND GROAN BUT STILL DO IT?

DID YOU ALSO KNOW ....
that the law (2002) does not require children to start school until the term after their 5th birthday?

The trouble is that some headteachers and governors imply that if children don't enrol when they are 4 – 'There might not be room at 5+' ...
UGH! What a lousy thing to do...

BUREAUCRAT'S BOSH

I am indebted to John Clare of the Daily Telegraph for these quotes (July 2003).

The profile, issued this year for the first time to the parents of 600,000 children at the end of reception year, is a 12 page multi-coloured booklet stamped with the logos of the Department of Education and the Qualifications and Curriculum Authority.

That's where money meant for classrooms goes!

It contains 117 statement boxes arranged in three tiers under six headings, plus a 650-word formulaic report. So, for a class of 30 children, the teacher must check **3510** boxes and churn out **20,000** words.

That's where teachers' time for teaching goes!

Examples of the statements to be checked are: *"Understands that people have different needs, views, cultures and beliefs that need to be treated with respect"* (personal, social and emotional development); *"Recognises a few familiar words"* *(communication, language and literacy)*; *"Relates addition to combining two groups, and subtraction to taking away"* (mathematical development);

"Builds and constructs with a wide range of objects" (knowledge and understanding of the world); *"Moves with confidence in a variety of ways, showing some awareness of space"* (physical development); and *"Explores colour, texture, shape, form and space in two or three dimensions"* (creative development).

In a host of European and USA Schools children are doing all these things – but it is called playing at home (or in the pre-school playgroup). They don't go to schools such as we have developed until 5 or even 6.

Do we really need 117 different ways to assess a five-year-old's development?

Parents and Teachers must summon up the courage to say NO!

Here are the 12 pages of education prattle I've been sitting up night after night doing ...instead of preparing lovely activities for your child the next day

PARENTS EVENING

Thanks a lot but really I don't want it. I'd rather have a useful chat

TARGETS
TESTS
PROGRESS
REPORTS

BE STRONG SPEAK OUT!

YES!

Quote from AN EXPERIMENT IN EDUCATION by Sybil Marshall:

Any attempt to use set schemes of work based on a rigid four year cycle with these living children would have been like trying to tie up water in a net or false-line.

What utter nonsense, what short sighted idiocy, what criminal waste of time it is for administrators in a central office continually to ask the teacher on the spot for bureaucratic evidence of his intention to teach! It must be supposed that they justify themselves by saying that they must have some tangible proof that the teacher is doing the job he is paid to do, but it is a negation of all the ideals of education that they should bring it down to this level. The motto of every chief education officer should be another quotation from Confucius:

If you suspect a man, do not employ him;
if you employ a man, do not suspect him.

9

What's the problem?

And what do we do about it?

The problem is that many teachers have forgotten, and Ofsted never accepted or perhaps never knew – **that young children are not miniature adults.**

Nor are they watered down eight year olds, nine year olds, or thirteen year olds – or thirty five year olds!

A five year old is **FIVE.**

He or she is five because she is five and not because she will soon be six or sixty six.

Many parents don't know this either – they seem to like the notion of Amanda Jane being dressed up as a 'Little Miss' or boys as 'Dad and his lad'.

Naturally enough the commercial world love this even more.

Too many parents are willing to swap their children's childhood for the pretentious 'glitz' of what was once a 'teenage culture'. Instead of childhood we see small children pushed into pseudo adult fashioned clothing, hair styles, gel, layers, foods, jewels, music, TV and pastimes of adulthood. It is terrible and embarrassing to behold. Many parents will argue:

"Oh, we don't want our children missing out".

This is a fib.

They do it because it makes THEM feel good!

Schools can make a similar mistake

The notion of children being small adults is often the standpoint of bad practice in schools.

The child becomes a consumer – commercially and educationally.

The notion of child development has all but disappeared from our teaching –as if, in curriculum terms, a six year old is simply a sixteen year old who has not lived quite so long.

Bernard Ashley, 2003

A POEM CALLED SCHOOL AT THREE

"Instead of letting them learn through doing things we will get them into sitting still, skills and targets."

'Send them to school when they're babies, teach them to sit and obey, childhood's as dead as a dodo and so is a birthright called play.'

CAN WE MAKE??

Can we make some good things?
Can we build some boats,
witches in their castles
and tigers munching goats?
Can we make some pattercakes?
Can we make some pies,
sloppy things and floppy things
and frogs with pebble eyes?
 Oh can we make some hot dogs,
 oh can we make clay meals?
Oh please...
 don't give us thumb pots –
 we want to make things real!

No, you can't. Now you are four we will learn facts and skills which one day you will thank me for having shown you.

PSEUDO CHILD WORK
An example of what I am talking about ...

All these are bogus.

You know, I know, and even the children know, that they did not really do these things.

The grown-ups did them.

The children helped (whatever that means).

The whole scenario is daft, but we see it all the time
WHY?
We asked Ms. Template from Smartstart Nursery Unit...

STATEMENT

"They can't do much when they are small and even though it's mostly the teacher's work, it gives them a sense of pride."

WELL YES WE HAD TO DO A LITTLE BIT TO HELP THEM.

OUR CLOCKS

ANSWER

Young children can do a billion things, **but they will do them differently** from grown-ups or other age groups. If we want them to do things that look like junior school work, then of course they can't. They are not ten and we are fooling ourselves to pretend they are.

It seems to me that many adults are ashamed of children under 5 or 6. They seem embarrassed by their 'natural' work, and fob them off with pseudo 'grown up stuff' that bears no relationship to who they are, and what age they are.

AIM OBJECTIVE TARGET ...
Today we explored texture and colour by sticking pasta on cardboard plates and spraying it all silver

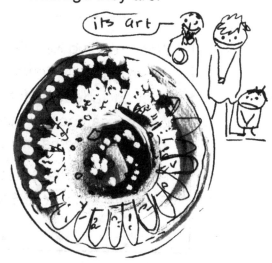

its art

IT IS NOT ART. IT IS NOT CREATIVE WORK.
It is unrelated to the child's stage of development.
IT'S PLAIN DAFT.

The 'THANK YOU FOR SAYING THESE THINGS' page ...
(Bernard Ashley and Philip Pullman)

The notion of child-development has all but disappeared from our pedagogy – as if, in curriculum terms, a six year old is simply a sixteen year old who hasn't lived quite so long. As a result, we now expect children to analyse books and poems before they've learned to enjoy them. Is this because analysis is easier to teach and test than enjoyment?

Bernard Ashley

When teachers are under pressure to get so many pupils to such-and-such point in order meet externally imposed targets they have to do things – for the sake of the school – that might not be things they'd do for the sake of children.

Philip Pullman

When reading Key Stages 1 - 3 of the National Lit. Strategy I wrote down the verbs used by the writers. They included reinforce, predict, check, discuss, identify, categorise, analyse, locate ... and so on. 71 different verbs by my count.

For the activities that came under the heading READING the word ENJOY did not come once.

Philip Pullman

**Quotes from *Meeting with the Minister*
National Centre for Language and Literacy 2003**

Particular thanks to Chris Powling!

Pretentious Ofsted requests...

For a number of years I spent much of my time writing units of work for adults studying for a BA or MA degree. During this time I learnt the jargon of assessment – aims objectives etc. – necessary to satisfy university quality control buffs and degree validation panels.

> Imagine my amazement when I discovered that the programmes plans for little children were equally complicated and constraining!

IT'S ABSOLUTELY BARMY!

Here for example is a sheet I found for children who were just enjoying doing some gardening.

Planning

Day 3	Stepping Stones/ learning goal	Activity	Adult role	Resources & Assessment focus
1. Personal, social and emotional development	Respecting other children and adults	See 4. Knowledge and understanding of the World and 5. Physical development	Ensure all children are included and observe the group	See 4. Knowledge and Understanding of the World and 5. Physical development
2. Knowledge and understanding of the world	Investigate materials by using senses	Filling plant pots with wet sand	Use capacity language with children	Plant pots,scoops, sand tray, water.
3. Physical development	Show increasing control	Pushing wheelbarrow up and down ramps	Discuss pushing and pulling with group	Wheelbarrows, ramps
4. Creative development	Work creatively making patterns	Collage activity continued	Introduce vocabulary to help children compare and discuss	Collage materials

In any good home or school, children will meet, encounter and come to terms with all these issues, in their own way, time and style. Of course the good teacher will be on hand to discuss, make, consolidate and help. We don't, however, require an agenda, a scheme or a curriculum in these early years! We are talking about five year olds. They do all this and tons more in real play.

Let's look at these pretentious Ofsted requests...

> **"to explore colour, texture, shape, form and space in two and also three dimensions"**

I know what they mean – I see it when children play but...

What pontificating blurb!

Why on earth do we use such silly jargon? Children have their own unique understanding of space, form and colour. It is an ability adult artists ENVY!

WE MUST NOT SACRIFICE CHILDREN'S EXPRESSION TO PLEASE OVERAMBITIOUS PARENTS OR OFSTED BOX TICKERS

Of course children need to learn things (even form, tone and texture!) but in a way suited to their stage of development. Not as pseudo junior or secondary pupils.

WRONG WAY

JOLLY TEMPLATES

COLOUR ME IN BOOK

Everyone watch carefully and see how we can do a lovely little cat

RIGHT WAY

PAINT

And then Tibby spat all the chewed up dinner all down Mummy's dress and then... and then...

We must never forget the fact that children have an innate and natural way of drawing: mark making (unless some adult has knocked it out of them).

It's their birthright.

All children possess it.

It's part of our/their cultural heritage.

All children, in all countries – throughout history – make marks, signs, symbols: 'DRAW'. They do it in their own way and don't need showing.

They do need encouragement and to feel that grown-ups are interested. Often adults will show different materials to draw on or with. Until the National Curriculum came along the sort of drawing seen in *Regio* exhibitions was all over the walls of our schools!!

LET'S LOOK AT THE SORT OF DEVELOPMENTAL ART CHILDREN SHOULD BE DOING...

This is the world your children are a part of. A privilege for you both to enjoy.

Do not keep it from them.

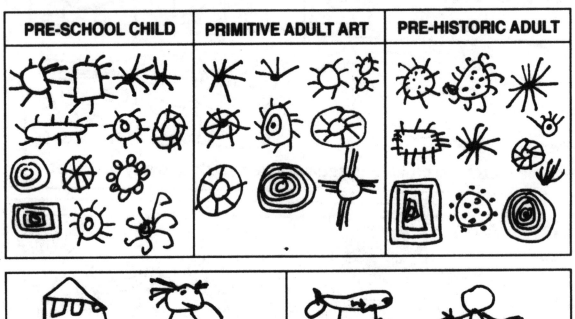

PRE-SCHOOL CHILD	PRIMITIVE ADULT ART	PRE-HISTORIC ADULT

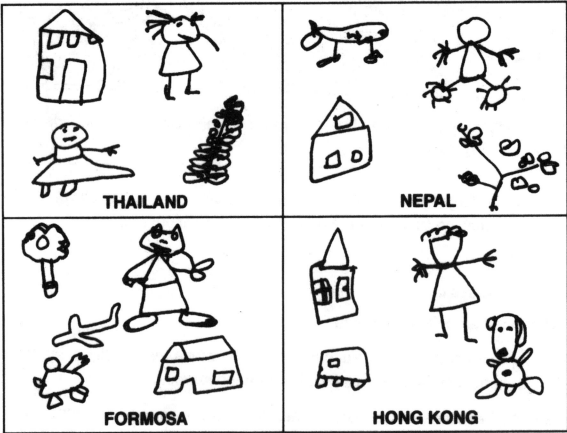

THAILAND

NEPAL

FORMOSA

HONG KONG

We find an amazing similarity of marks between those scratched on cave walls, those made by early Egyptian children and those of today from Iraq and China to Africa and Basingstoke!

As children have a natural delight and inclination to make drawings in this way... then let us rejoice in it. **And not replace it by horrid 'measurable' adult art.**

Are you aware of the stages children encounter as they develop concepts through drawing?

There are numerous books explaining the development of children's drawings. Such books are lengthy and detailed. All I can manage here is the briefest of outlines — enough I hope to generate further reading.

I UNDERLINE THE CRIME AGAINST CHILDHOOD IF SUCH STAGES SHOULD BE BY-PASSED.

Don't do silly scribbles, darling. Daddy's bought you a colouring-in book.

WE PAINT MODERN ART

At our school we don't paint
    like children.
We paint like real artists.
We paint proper pictures
    of water-gardens we have
    never seen
    smelt
    felt
    or fallen into.
We paint them like Frenchmen
    ten times our age
    painted water-gardens
    ninety years ago.
Sometimes we paint Kandinskys
or draw Miros with biros.
We also do other Famous Artists,
    Hues
    Tones
    Shade
    and Texture,
and of course Sunflower.

STAGE OUTLINES

About 18 months Kinaesthetic	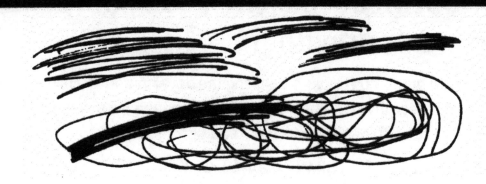
	Joy of feeling, fingers on steamy windows, soapsuds on floor... crayon ...chalk; a windscreen sort of movement.
2 years The Scribbling Stage	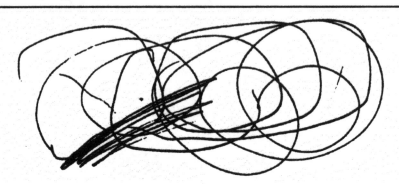
	Marks still showing, round and round – it's the feeling, not the sight of the mark. Pencil stays on paper. Still kinaesthetic.
Scribbles which are the beginning of the human figure.	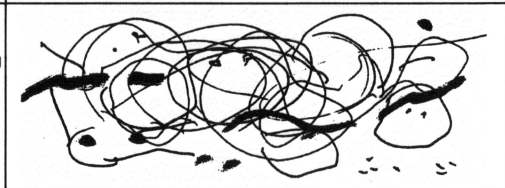
	The 'kinaesthetic feeling' is less important. The child is willing to interrupt feeling... i.e. remove crayon from surface. Dots. Breaks.
The 'talking as they draw' stage. They begin to name their scribbles.	
	Enthusiastic scribbles. Chalk often comes off paper.. dots... dashes... pauses, stop/start drawing.

Child talks as he/she draws. Looks at scribbles and names them more clearly.	
	Human figure begins to appear. Eyes, mouth, nose, arms.
Me - mummy, daddy, dog, mandala shapes	
	Often family people. Legs, hair – more details
Stage of Confidence in drawing anything	
	Other representations appear. Not human: trees, suns, cars. Things they've seen: boats, caravans, elephants.

This is known as the pre-schematic stage – about 4 - 7 years old – when people, cars, suns, trees, birds, whatever, seem to look different every time they are drawn. Creatures still have human faces. Children are ego-centric.

"I'm central – things are like me."

THIS PRE-SCHEMATIC STAGE

This pre-schematic stage is the best of all! And it belongs to you and your children.

It is a wonderland to behold – pure magic. Children draw their world with uninhibited abandon ... people, pets, houses, flowers – run, fly, dance and are seen to perform in arrangements of line and colour pulsating with energy and invention.

Colours, tones, textures and forms vibrate in compositions which render our own feeble attempts as nothing.

"I play my world of real believe
I play it everyday
and teachers stand and watch me
but don't know what to say.

They give me diagnostic tests,
they try out reading schemes,
but none of them will ever
know the colour of my dreams."

UNLESS.... OF COURSE...

Unless of course an adult steps in and ruins everything by short circuiting childhood and handing out their answer.

CHILD ART

I want to paint sunshine,
moonbeams and stars.
I want to paint hedgehogs
and rainbows in jars.
I want to paint laughter,
clouds filled with rain,
music and songbirds
again and again.
I don't want to paint Monets,
Miros or tones
textures and shadings,
peppers and bones.
I want to paint paintings
of things that I see,
grandmas and cuddles
belonging to me.

It is not only in 'art' that children are fobbed off with skills/techniques and activities alien to their stage of development and understanding. It happens all the time. Just read government documents - incentives - directives etc. 'Learning' is confused with something called PRODUCT (i.e. measurable). PROCESS is all too often ignored. Read through teachers' plans. Facts to be taught dominate ... HOW they will be taught conveniently skated over, other than tell, write and test.

PROCESS NOT PRODUCT

Your child is passing through a specific and very important stage of learning. It is called the *pre-schematic stage*. If we don't get this stage right it will hamper further development. So we work hard to get it right! And we ask for your understanding and support.

Your children are at a stage where the *process* of doing things –

LOOKING, SEEKING, FINDING, FEELING, INVESTIGATING etc.

is far more important than the end product sought by some parents and Ofsted. Whilst obviously being on hand to assist children our staff do not, at this stage, believe in your child making bogus objects.

- plates with faces
- filling in teacher's outlines
- template colouring in
- noddy ducks... or copying Monets!

Such activities are a denial of our children's abilities to sort, find, invent, talk, discuss and think for themselves.

So, your children probably won't bring many finished objects home. Their work – or *the process of their work* – might look messy, scribbly or completely unrecognisable to us – but to your children it is utterly meaningful, and an essential part of their mental and physical growth and development.

Please honour – please respect – your child's own way of thinking. It might seem unusual, but it is their birthright. It is the **foundation** upon which they will build all future understanding.

We want your children to enjoy childhood. There is no evidence that early pressure results in success ... learning must be meaningful and enjoyable.

I haven't learnt my spellings
and I'm sobbing off to sleep.
My pillows wet and sticky
and it's like it every week.
I have not learnt my ten words
and tomorrow there's a test ...
flowers on my duvet
...failure on my chest

NO THANK YOU OFSTED!
Not for our children.

Introducing
MISTER 'AH! BUT.....'

"If children do their own things, the results will be messy and scribbly. Parents don't want that."

ANSWER

Of course young children's work is wildly different – messy, scribbly – unrecognisable. But it isn't scribbly or unrecognisable ...

to them

To children it is as meaningful as your O.U. essay, carefully decorated room or correctly filled in tax return.

The work on this page is as meaningless as you copying down my tax returns or copying out Einstein's theory of relativity. It is adult work. It is a 35 year olds! Not a 4 or 5 year olds.

Who are we kidding?

HEY – *just a minute!*

When parents send their children to a school or nursery or whatever, they want to see something for their money. If the teachers 'help and direct the work' (do most of it) then it looks good. Parents want to show aunties and uncles how well their children are doing.

"Dressing them up in proper little uniforms, desks and sitting in rows helps – but they need proper things to take home. If children don't produce smart work, parents will send them to the pushy place down the road".

ANSWER

No, they won't.

Parents are not daft. They know when it's the children's work and when it isn't. They know when they are being taught as children and when they are not.

If we or you explain to parents that we have a responsibility to put children's natural and personal development at the top of the list they will understand.

Tell the parents how you work with their children. Once they know they will support you. They are on your side. They want the best as well!

We must not pretend that young children are like other, older, children. We have to teach them in a special way. Teachers of this age group will know about stages of development and will be doing things that might not have a product.

Beware of schools where teachers 'do it for them'. Or teach art 'theory'.

If people say that it is good to fill in squirrel pictures because one day they will have to be able to draw squirrels and that this is getting them ready,

THEN SAY THIS....

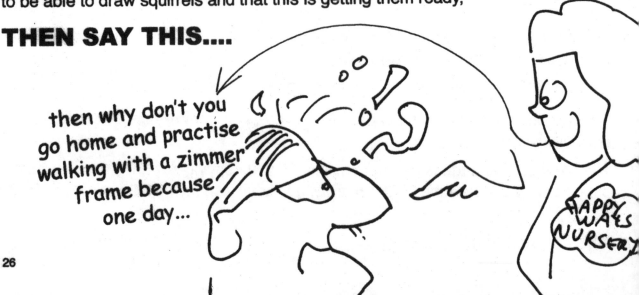

then why don't you go home and practise walking with a zimmer frame because one day...

Many schools pressurise children from 3 years onwards - in a manner never seen before ...

I see children's 'success' and 'achievement' charts displayed on classroom walls!

I see ridiculous reports or progress breakdowns about children who should be playing in the sand and painting pink panderellos in the spring of their life.

I see pseudo-secondary school 'lessons'.

I see children being taught to read before they are anywhere near ready – they simply learn to bark out words.

I see play, imagination and childhood thrown aside in a supposedly triumphant race to a mecca of false success.

I've only been at school three days and already I am bringing reading books home

Come on son try another page...

GLAD I'M A CAT.

I even attend courses entitled "Celebrating Success"!!

I wasn't sorry to see Estelle Morris, Blunkett, Woodhead, Baker and company go. They made children's lives boring and often miserable in an attempt to bring success to themselves and their political party.

HOW MANY TIMES HAVE YOU HEARD POLITICAL OUTBURSTS BY EDUCATION MINISTERS LIKE THIS?

BUT MY CHILDREN FIND IT BORING.

"and now standards are rising..."
"and with our new funding..."
"and with our new initiatives..."
"and already a 97.932% success rate has been measured..."

A POEM FOR ANYONE WHO STILL SUBJECTS CHILDREN TO SATS

Once I dreamed in colours,
> built castles in the sky,
> watched dragons building love nests
> and angels in the sky.
I wrote of singing serpents,
> touched the morning dew
> saw a goldfish dancing,
> and painted apples blue.
But now I dream of magnets,
> booster groups,
> and words,
> apostrophes
> and clauses
> and hear no singing birds.
My teacher's world is worksheets,
> objectives,
> lists and aims...
I have no dreams or sunshine –
> and my pillow's stained
> with rains.

B B C News

The Today Programme

Mr P Dixon
30 Cheriton Road
Winchester
SO22 SAX   June 3rd 2004

Dear Mr Dixon

It was very kind of you to send me 'Let Me Be'. On the basis of what I have read, I think I agree with pretty much everything you say. That, believe me, is rare.

Yours sincerely,

JOHN HUMPHRYS

Children even go home with homework –
- ■ word lists
- ■ spelling to learn
- ■ pages to read...

... not because they
LOVE BOOKS AND WORDS...

(oh that they did!)
but in order to do well in future tests!

Headteachers are under more pressure when it comes to league tables than Glenn Hoddle, ever is or ever was.

"We must be seen to be doing OK. I know its not right but what else can I do?"

"Maybe if we gave them honework, things to learn for tests. it might help a bit..."

Many pressurise staff with aims, objectives, assessments, attainments, forward planning. Such bunkum will thrill Ofsted, but it will also knock the stuffing out of good teachers. "I didn't come into the profession to do this".

HOW SHOULD CHILDREN BE TAUGHT?

Oddly enough it's easy to explain.
Not so easy to do.

Margaret Donaldson summed it up for us in her excellent book, *Children's Minds*:

> Your children <u>do not learn</u> by first mastering the skills...
>
> ✦ ✦ ✦
>
> They learn in meaningful contexts ... by trial and error and furthermore this learning should be enjoyable and rewarding.
>
> ✦ ✦ ✦

If you read no more of this book than this quote then you are home and dry.

IT SAYS IT ALL.

It is all so obvious.
So simple. So straightforward.

But sadly largely ignored by Ofsted type people.

Read the first two lines again...

Phew!

Sounds horrific – the idea of skills not being the first thing in learning!

But it is so true!

SKILLS ARE IMPORTANT

Of course they are! But they are meaningless and ineffectual if taught at the wrong time, in the wrong way.

Oh yes!

It is great for teachers or parents to boast that Hannah can do this or that aged 2, 3 or 4.

We might feel terrific. Hannah might feel terrific, but if the skill is not set in a meaningful context then like the flower in the bible:

It springs up, but withers and dies because there is no root.

HOW CHILDREN LEARN IN A MEANINGFUL CONTEXT
Let's take reading as an example...

I love the sounds of words
I love the feel of books
I love the sight of books
I love the pictures
I love the words
I love the stories
I love the stories repeated
I love them being told
I love parts of them being read
I love lots of them read
I love the way they are read
I love to join in
I love to say the words
I can't stop wanting books
I can't stop joining in
I want to know what that word says
I want to know what another word says
I am in love with books
I want books more and more
I am a real reader.

Because I really like reading – not word barking – I am a reader for life

We are real readers!

I am not a barker of words! I am not someone who has been turned off reading. Please don't spoil my joy and enthusiasm by slogging phonics at me too early and making the book to take home a turn off instead of a pleasure.

If we make something enjoyable like this, then children will learn. not just reading, but everything else.

RELUCTANT READER

Phonics are awful,
phonics aren't fun!
I did them with teacher,
I did them with Mum.
I didn't ask to 'build up',
I wanted just to share
the pictures and the pages,
the words about the bears.
I only wanted wonder
but they told me I was
wrong...
    they only gave me
        phonics
        and never sang
        the song.

OK! I DO AGREE THAT PHONICS ARE USEFUL, BUT ONLY IN THE CONTEXT OF ENJOYING READING REAL BOOKS, NOT AS AN END IN THEMSELVES!

THE ODE OF A DOOMED READER

LEARNING THE WORDS
(so the school can get a good report)

I have not learnt my five words ...
    they're broken in my head,
    bits of 'would'
    and 'should be'
    fighting round my bed.
Geoffrey Ridden knows them,
    the others know them too,
    they can do the big ones
    and tricky words like 'glue'.
But I get stuck on all words –
I don't know 'knew' from 'new' –
my words are made of teardrops
    and I'm not as good as you.

LEARNING THROUGH ENJOYMENT

Learning because you want to learn...

Wanting to obtain skills because you can't do what you love doing without them...

I have cited reading as an example, but as I say the same principle applies to all areas of learning

Talking and walking probably being the premier examples.

Who tests and measures, sets aims and objectives for talking?

Unless dummies are shoved into mouths to keep children quiet, or they are never spoken to, it just happens **in the meaningful context called family life.** You learn to crawl or walk because you want to touch the cat or get the biscuit!

SADLY....

Sadly enough I think the church has all too often been the culprit of teaching children badly i.e. not in a meaningful context.

The "you might not like or understand this now... but one day you'll appreciate what I am telling you" approach.

In my road everyone went to Sunday School and nearly everyone discontinued church as soon as they

HOLST: The right time to learn anything is because you can't get by without knowing it.

grew up – in other words, were not made to go! The message – or lesson – of the church was wonderful. The teachers were sincere, but the learning of texts, the recitation of hymns and prayers, colouring of biblical pictures wasn't the way to generate understanding in 5 - 11 year old London kids.

Or any others.

OK, someone will always say:
> *It worked for me.*

FINE! But what about the other 90%?

There is certainly some benefit **in almost any teaching method**, for someone. But that's not good enough.

Teaching in an enjoyable and rewarding manner in a meaningful context has the maximum benefit for every child.

We must plan activities which are 'winners'. Things to do that we know kids love. Often this will happen outside. Having engaged them in something they enjoy... then we introduce the 'learning in a context' fact or skill.

PLEASE READ MARGARET'S STATEMENT
AGAIN
AND YET AGAIN

> **Children do not learn by first mastering the skills. They learn in a meaningful context and furthermore that learning should be enjoyable and rewarding.**

That will go down like a lead balloon at St. Wonderstart's Nursery staff meeting!

But it is true!

Educationalists do not say that skills don't matter .. but they do say that it is not the way in which we begin our teaching. "Children don't learn by first mastering skills."

Skills are a very attractive way of teaching for some people... because

- **they are testable**
- **they are measurable**
- **they will impress Ofsted**
- **they will impress some parents**

"Emma can count to 154, recognise 69 words, write her name and half her address, mix yellow and blue to make green, balance on one foot for 9 minutes, use scissors to cut a circle, sit silently and sieve. She can also name a foreign country and sing in tune, say her colours and use a thin brush."

But there is no evidence that this 'Early Skills Start' will lead to the child becoming a clever scholar or person.

'And the flowers sprang up but withered and faded for there was no real root...'

There is the terrible possibility that early 'hothouse' teaching, as apparent early success, will only lead to a hollow form of understanding, resulting before long in disappointment and even trauma.

OFSTED TEACHING

I can tick boxes
write missions
and aims –
list my objectives,
targets and names ...
    I can plan lessons,
    worksheets to do,
    tests and assessments
    and everything new.
My file is a triumph,
an inspector's delight,
in S.A.T.S. and achievement,
everything's right.
They call me professional,
I'm Ofsted adored,
but don't ask the children –
    they're weary
    and bored.

I am indebted to PETER NEWSAM for an article written circa 1980 in the Times Educational Supplement.

In particular, examination fever is leading to ever more fatuous and expensive efforts to measure the immeasurable. In the 1970s Sir Alex Clegg set us laughing at some items in the Educational Assessment Program in the state of Michigan:

"By the end of pre-kindergarten experience 90 per cent of all children will demonstrate their recognition of at least three of the five basic emotions: fear, anger, sadness, joy and love (in self and others) as measured by a future Michigan Education Assessment Program (MEAP) battery of tests.

By the end of the third grade children will create vocal or instrumental accompaniments to songs using combinations of melodic, harmonic or rhythmic patterns as measured by a minimum criteria (sic) or an Objective Reference Test. Example: while the class sings the chorus 'Oh Susanna', the child plays the tambourine any way he chooses."

There's freedom for you. But today we have no grounds for trans-Atlantic laughter. We have our home-grown hilarities.

As for teachers, the prodding is developing into increasingly complex forms of accountability for all, with the prospect of cash prizes for a few thrown in. This is utter folly. When the young Michaelangelo went to paint the ceiling of the Sistine Chapel he was not accompanied by a note suggesting that he would paint better if given an extra height allowance. The note – a favourite of Sir Alec's was written by someone who understood human nature. It read:

"The bearer of these presents is the sculptor Michaelangelo. His nature is such that he needs to be drawn out by kindness and encouragement, but if love be shown him and he be treated kindly he will accomplish things which will make the whole world wonder."

I TAKE THE LIDS OFF CHILDREN ...
WHEREAS OTHERS KEEP THEM ON.
Chizek, *circa 1920*

Hopefully these two statements will form a useful lead into the section of this booklet devoted to **CREATIVITY**.

LEARNING MUST BE ENJOYABLE

It must be part of 'play'.
It is through play that children learn.

Play is not a fooling 'mucking around' activity ... it is through play that children learn to understand themselves and their world.

Educators call it *forming concepts*.

It is essential that in these early years children are able to form concepts of space, time, shape, fear, light, dark, words, friendship, numbers, happiness, safety, sadness etc. in an enjoyable and understandable manner.

Unfortunately they cannot learn these things by merely being told or instructed. Education (unfortunately!) is not quite as easy as that. Young children learn by experience. They learn through doing things, and the way to offer the DOING EXPERIENCE that leads to the LEARNING is through play.

They do this naturally, but we can add to this natural play and make their experiences and their learning that much richer.

Some few years ago the boss Ofsted man declared at a conference at Warwick University that he saw no place for creativity in the Primary Years. So he shut it all down.

Naturally enough it withered and faded, but recently (2004) it is returning! Or so I am told. I am not so sure!

> **I am very suspicious. Why the sudden concern about creativity? I believe Ofsted types don't really know what it is anyway and will fob teachers off with something bogus.**

Read the awful foundation profile stuff – see what I mean? They are already confusing creative thinking with 'tone, texture, space and hue'. They can't even see that tools and techniques are not creative in themselves.

A skill (e.g printing) is not creative in itself, it is what the child does with it that's creative.

CREATIVITY what is it?

Many parents and inspectors won't really know much about creativity.

So long as children are:
    'making things'
    or 'playing'
    or 'being imaginative'
    and particularly if children are doing what they call 'close observational drawing' or 'experimenting'...
    learning hues and tones and colour mixing
    or even copying a Monet ...
        they will be happy.

If we do things with children that are not easily measured or have no obvious end result or skill base, we are likely to be misunderstood or even criticised.

So we have to be able to explain the principles of creativity underlying our work with children.

We need to speak out with authority and confidence.

Being creative involves THINKING. This thinking is not always the imaginative or fantasising kind of thought. It is often quite a factual and logical kind of thinking.

Creativity can be as firmly based in science or maths activities as the arts, but obviously the 'arts' area is an extremely fertile field in which to exercise such thinking.

TELL PARENTS & OFSTED THIS

Whatever your children become as adults they need to **FIRE ON ALL CYLINDERS,** In other words they won't totally fulfil their role as butcher, baker, candlestick maker, mum, dad, artist, accountant or whatever...

IF THEY ARE UNABLE TO THINK CREATIVELY.

Schools are selling our children short if creative activity is not an inherent part of daily school work

Teachers must explain to people ...

Because we have a responsibility to your child, we teach in a creative and imaginative way – we refuse to sell your child short...

We spend time every single day exercising their creative thinking... a lot of time! We also refuse to trick your children into producing the bogus creative work often encouraged by people who don't understand what creativity is and why it is so important.

... all about creativity

Having stated very strongly that children ought to have plenty of opportunities to exercise their creative and imaginative potential, the reader has every right to expect a helpful and illuminating definition of the term and its processes.

I agree.

The problem is that it demands a great deal of writing to explain the essentials of creativity and how such thinking can be exercised and developed.

In fact it needs a book of its own – or three or four or five books!

Obviously I can give an academic reading list and libraries can supply the volumes. Some folk might relish the study, but I try to be a realist. People who read this publication – parents, teachers, helpers etc. – are not going to pursue an academic and lengthy avenue of creative studies reading. All I can hope to do is to offer a basic and straightforward outline of the creative process. It is not meant to be anything more than a helpful guide or introduction.

I begin with a poem and an article I wrote in 1985 and I will extend it with a range of further ideas and comments.

THE COLOUR OF MY DREAMS

I'm really a rotten reader, the worst in all the class,
the sort of rotten reader that makes you want to laugh.
I'm last in all the readin' tests, my score's not on the page
and when I read to teacher she gets in such a rage.

She says I cannot form my words, she says I can't build up
and that I don't know phonics – and don't know c-a-t from k-u-p.
They say that I'm dysploksik (that's a word they've just found out)
...but when I get some plasticine I know what that's about.

I make these scary monsters, I draw these secret lands
and get my hair all sticky and paint on all me hands.
I make these super models, I build these smashing towers
that reach up to the ceiling and take me hours and hours.

I paint these lovely pictures in thick green drippy paint
that gets all on the carpet and makes the cleaners faint.
I build great magic forests, weave bushes out of string
and paint pink panderellos and birds that really sing.

I play my world of real believe, I play it every day
and people stand and watch me, but don't know what to say.
They give me diagnostic tests, they try out special schemes,
but none of them will ever know the colour of my dreams.

*I am nonplussed by teachers' obsession with stuffy classrooms.
Even if 'outside' is only asphalt or boring grass... any teacher
worth their salt will invent purposeful activities. Even if it's
only planting spuds or chalking asphalt-eating monsters.
OK... books, papers, pencils are not easy outside, but learning
is not utterly dependent upon these things, is it?*

MORE ABOUT CREATIVITY

I wonder what your response is to the poem on the previous page? At a guess I suppose many people's reaction would be: "Poor child! I KNOW splashing about with clay and paint is important ... but it is even more important to be successful at the basic skills of life."

If we are perfectly honest with ourselves I think many of us would rate creative activity as being well down the list of parent's wishes and aspirations for their children.

Or, put another way – if he or she is going to be bad at anything then let it be art and the creativity stuff.

Most people think art doesn't matter very much. After all we can get on without being very good at dough modelling – but just try making your way in the world being illiterate! In the brief space that I have at my disposal I would like to make points which could assist both workers and parents to gain insight into the value of painting pink panderellos and making bushes out of string...

To begin with I think it is essential that parents realise that art making is an intellectual activity.

When children are working creatively then they are THINKING. As a lecturer in a College concerned with Teacher Education I spent a great deal of time working with experienced teachers in situations very similar to those encountered in any good playgroup creative activity area.

My teachers worked hard (as our children do), but unlike small children they were more easily able to articulate their feelings about building towers and making birds out of string and scrap.... and their response was always the same: "We find this mentally exhausting".

Probably their knees ached. Probably they found making junk giants physically exhausting – but that was not their "complaint". Time after time they cited their exhaustion as being a mental one. A thinking one.

So – when teachers and helpers ask children to make, build and invent, they are demanding that they exercise THINKING. The child in the poem couldn't read, but he was obviously well able to think.

Having explained that creative work is thinking time, it is important to point out that it exercises a kind of thinking somewhat different from the type of thinking a child might be using when she is reading, or writing or adding up or learning facts.

It is not a more important kind of thinking. It is not a less important kind of thinking. It simply involves a different area of the brain.

If we can explain creative work as an intellectual activity, then maybe parents, inspectors etc. will see it (probably for the first time) as having a respectability in terms of education. We can go further because research has shown quite clearly that an ability to work/think creatively has as much relevance to the sciences, technology etc. as it has to the arts. In other words a person who can think in a rounded sense i.e. using all areas of the brain, will function that much better at whatever they might be doing, be it science, maths or art. Might I suggest two things in conclusion?

Firstly, parents should be more supportive to those schools which are trying to develop the 'whole child' by offering plenty of opportunities for creative and imaginative development. Support them all 100%!

Be grateful to those stalwart helpers who are willing to make the effort to present clay, dough, paint, junk, fabrics, wood, strings, mud and water to your children. It is certainly EASIER for them not to. It is because they are informed and really care about YOUR CHILD'S DEVELOPMENT that they make the effort, and next time your child gets painty or muddied – rejoice that he or she is having the opportunity! They are receiving real education.

My second plea is directed towards those teachers who confuse child art with their own. They themselves have a willingness to make and build, stick and glue, paint and draw, but they suffer from a lack of confidence in the validity of their children's work. They want to do it (or at least half of it) for them!

We see this every time the children walk back home with a teacher-invented toilet roll Father Christmas, table decoration, calendar, templated picture or filled in outline. It has as much to do with creativity as me copying out Wordsworth's poem *Daffodils* and claiming to have written it myself. It is ridiculous and, in terms of creativity, indefensible (though you might find other values if you look hard enough).

Please don't be ashamed of childhood creativity. Please don't deny your child the opportunity of doing his or her own things in the way that is their birthright.

In the words of J.A. Hadfield:
Far from being a gramophone record whose function is simply to record and reproduce that which we as adults care to record... the child is an internal combustion engine capable of spontaneous combustion.'

So fetch the clay, get the glue and watch the pink panderellos fly.

For your children's sake.

WHY NOT PHOTOCOPY OR SNIP BITS OUT FOR A PARENTS' NEWSLETTER? THEY NEED TO BE TOLD. SO DO OFSTED.

AMMUNITION - USEFUL FACTS

All too often, loving, kind and concerned parents avoid nurseries and schools where creative and imaginative work is an important part of daily life. They prefer Ofsted type 3R places... because they are easy to understand with their scores, measurements, skills etc.

If we stand up for the child and offer them the creative life they deserve, then we must be able to justify our actions. We must be able to explain our beliefs, to have the right words for Ofsted: **The Ammunition.**

No...I am not doing what you expected because we are doing something much much better. Let me explain.

Daily News
DAVID BELL SAYS IT IS TIME FOR TEACHERS TO **SEIZE THE INITIATIVE!**

We must avoid being vague. We must justify our work in cold clear terms.

WE MUST NOT TALK IN NON-EDUCATIONALIST WAYS – LIKE THIS:

Oh, they're having a lovely time at the printing and painting table... If you're finished do another... they just love experimenting and expressing themselves.

It's all such fun, running and splashing...

WORDS LIKE FUN AND 'EXPERIMENTING' ARE NOT GOOD ENOUGH FOR PARENTS & OFSTED.

WE MUST HAVE THE RIGHT WORDS. READ ON ⟶

The Silver Toilet Roll...

In 1978 I wrote a book entitled *The Silver Toilet Roll*. Within the book I presented ammunition so that if inspectors or parents ever questioned the validity or meaning of creative work, teachers would have the answers.

Of course there is nothing wrong with experimenting and investigating, printing or dressing up and finding, mixing and making. But if we (as I hope) devote a large proportion of the child's day to such work we need to justify the time expenditure successfully. We need strong clear facts at our finger tips.

> I wish you'd hurry up and tell us what these important facts are!

> How do we find the right words for parents and for school inspectors?

ANSWERS - well, here they are!

You have three choices:

1. Obtain *Creative and Mental Growth* by Viktor Lowenfelt (Macmillan, New York) from your library and read it carefully. It is long, profound and excellent.

2. Purchase *Silver Toilet Roll* from me*. It is short, quick, helpful, but not profound. It is a quick and useful read.

3. Read the next pages of this book as a helpful introduction. They won't define creativity, but they will enable you to stand up to the slings and arrows of unbelievers. They will give you the words to say!

> * £5 p & p included (for UK)
> *Cheques and orders to*
> Peche Luna
> 30 Cheriton Road
> Winchester SO22 5AX
> Tel. 01962 854607

Creativity

Getting it

in the early years

66 Creative work is not merely a question of playing with things, of randomness and chance. It has much to do with serious and sustained effort. Often at the highest levels of absorption and intensity. 99

Gulbenkian Report

PETER DIXON SAYS:

Creativity isn't a vague sort of 'artsy' gift or talent given by God to the favoured few. It is an ability inherent within us all. If it is not exercised it will wither and fade... and if children are denied the necessary time and opportunities to develop this right of birth it will be lost. I often encounter very young schoolchildren whose creative abilities are already stunted or impoverished forever.

This is our fault, not theirs.

Background

Until the mid-fifties/early sixties, the word creativity was hardly used in the context of early years education. It was a back burner word in terms of schooling. A word rarely used.

Then along came the space race and a huge input by the USA in research and development programmes. From this input the terms 'creativity' and 'creative thinking' rose like a phoenix.

Researchers began to cite creativity as an essential element in thinking styles and patterns of scientists and technological gurus. No longer was it sufficient to have three Phds or two double firsts in rocketry or ballistics... it was necessary to be able to think creatively as well! Suddenly the word became extremely respectable. It was lifted from the grime and seediness of the artist's garret or musician's den and placed upon its own rather fine pedestal.

Everything had (all at once) to be creative. I expect you remember: creative writing, creative cookery, creative architecture, creative styling, creative accountancy and creative gardening...

I recall the government happily paying me to go to London University, with a handsome grant and all fares paid, to do a one year Creativity Course. It had gained respectability.

American research funds had revealed that the ways of thinking associated with the processes of creativity enriched and enhanced the world of science as richly as the arts.

MEN AND WOMEN NEEDED TO FIRE ON ALL CYLINDERS

What was it that they discovered?
enquires Sir Boyse-Games, Deputy Head of Pinhole Beacon Primary School.

The fascinating fact is that their research into creativity was conducted with reference to adults. Why were some adults more creative or imaginative than others? A list was complied by one research programme into what factors seemed to be a part of the way in which creative adults thought, behaved, performed, acted ... **AND DID THINGS.**

I have listed these things – not all but most – on the next page and I intend to use them as the focus of our thinking.

What are these things creative adults do rather well?

Here are a few important ones;

1. environmental awareness
2. fluency of ideas
3. flexibility
4. self confidence
5. originality
6. redefinition
7. combining
8. sensitivity to problems

Please don't cringe, it isn't as awful as it sounds.

LET'S LOOK AT THEM IN TURN

Remember we are talking about adults – they were the ones 'investigated' but as I unfold them please think of the small children in your care. I suggest that children are naturally like this – from birth! I suggest that as you read about each attribute you are likely to say:

Hey, that's just what kids are like anyway, when they are playing or whatever.

LET'S LOOK ⟶

> The sculptor Sam Smith was asked why he built his wooden dancing ladies and lions in sailing boats... His answer was glorious.
>
> **"I believe in doing the unnecessary with love".** So do our children, if we allow them.

1. ENVIRONMENTAL AWARENESS

Creative people are the sort of people who are extra interested in the world around them. They pick, poke, proddle, listen, hear, ask, taste, touch, feel, smell, peer at, stare at, find, discover, collect. They look at the strange, the new - they ask, they enquire...

Have you ever found a child NOT like this?

2. FLUENCY OF IDEAS

Creative people are the sort of people who use things in all sorts of different ways. They might read the newspaper, but will equally swat flies, wrap fish 'n' chips, light fires, catch slugs. Children will use a biro top to pick teeth or nose, gnaw to cut teeth, fill with dribble, whistle through, print red circles on arm, make pinging noises with and to occasionally fit on to a pen! "Don't do that with your toothbrush, David."

Have you ever found a child NOT like this?

3. FLEXIBILITY

Creative people are flexible in their day to day lives. If they are doing something and it goes awry then they happily "go with the flow". If the paint is lumpy then they will call the wall 'textured'! If the sponge cake goes soggy and flat – then they will make it into a scrummy trifle. I saw a little girl knock the whole pot of water over her painting of mummy in a blue dress.

Never mind, Mummy can be in a swimming pool now...

YEA!

Have you ever found a child NOT like this?

48

4. SELF-CONFIDENCE

Creative adults will nearly always have a go at things – even if they have not the necessary skills. Take a trombone into a classroom, a mono-cycle or some juggling balls. "Who thinks they can play/ride/juggle with these?"

There will be a forest of waving hands.

5. ORIGINALITY

Originality is defined as "uncommonness of sensory response" – **Doing it differently from the way other people do it.**

Surely the children we teach are the absolute masters of this one!

6. COMBINING

Creative people seem to have an ability to join together all sorts of seemingly unrelated bits and pieces and make something "complete and whole" out of them. E.g. Picasso's bicycle saddle with handlebars which framed a magnificent bull's head; Schwitter's bus tickets and cigarette packets.

Or the script of Inspector Morse or Frost. It all seems 'bitty and confused', but in the end it is all neatly resolved into something we understand.

Creative people are good at things like that – and not just in 'Art'

When Alexander Fleming's experiment went wrong, weeks of work were wasted. But instead of saying: "Oh dear everything has been ruined"... he said: "Oh dear everything has been ruined, but I wonder what this strange thing growing in its place is? I will examine it instead."

**Thank God he did –
for the thing that went wrong turned out to be...**

PENICILLIN

Books say penicillin was discovered accidentally. Not so! It was discovered because a scientist thought creatively. He thought flexibly. The thing he was doing went wrong so he said to himself:

"Even though this isn't what I aimed for (planned)... I will go along with it .

When Liza or Darren are building something and it doesn't work out, do we encourage them to think creatively, i.e. flexibly or do we just allow them to walk away?

> **When we sort out things for creative activities have we got what creativity IS in our mind – what it is we are developing? Or are we just hoping they make something that looks OK?**

Today we will do a collage. Lola sticks on the cotton wool clouds, Ben the toilet roll lighthouse and Emma the cardboard rocks.

A seaside picture

Obviously the picture will be a success. The children will learn to follow instructions. The children will practice cutting, sticking, learning to share... being careful etc., etc.

But one thing they won't experience is their CREATIVE THINKING.

One hour later... # NEAT BUT POINTLESS

The children have been robots sticking on the pieces selected by the adult. Neat work but creatively sterile.

MESSY BUT MEANINGFUL

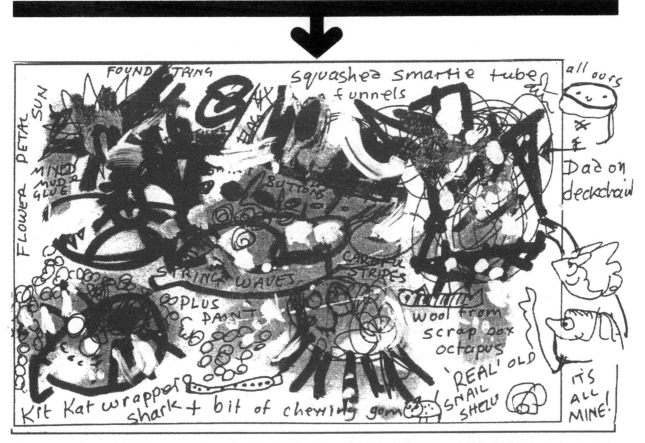

I've found... this, I've fixed it to that... I've wound it round and hooked it on to...
Messy, but the result is that of creative thinking.

I believe...

I believe that in some schools children do still enjoy opportunities for genuinely creative experiences and activities. That's good news. I do see children playing very purposefully with sand, mud, water, clay and sticks. I see camps being built, magic spells, dressing up and dressing downs. The excellent teachers who set up opportunities of this kind are to be congratulated – but I expect many of them are willing to accept the fact that they are doing these valuable things almost intuitively.

That's fine

I would hate to see teachers planning to do some flexible thinking work or setting up some fluency exercises.

An awful thought!

But I do think it is important for teachers, helpers and parents to be aware that there is a process and content to creativity.

It isn't an ether in the air that defies explanation.

Creativity has a firm identity and we must recognise its processes and honour its presence.

This second world

> Robert Witkin *The Intelligence of Feeling:*
>
> There is a world that exists beyond the child. A world that exists whether he or she exists, or not.
>
> The child needs to know about this world, move in it and manage himself or herself in it.

BUT!!! (I have deliberately extracted his final statement)

> But there is another world of his own sensations and feelings. He shares the former world with others. He shares this second world with no-one.

This is the world all too often excluded from our children's education.

Creativity today

Sadly very few people in education today understand the structure and processes of creativity. So long as triple mounted pictures adhere to the walls and children appear in painty shirts turned back to front at gluey tables –

All is well.

That is why I made a rather formal list of creativity factors. I dislike isolating such words from their context... but in a gentle and certainly not recorded manner, I hope parents and teachers will from time to time glance through the listed factors of creativity. I hope that as they watch children pursue varied activities they will ask themselves whether or not the children are REALLY BEING CREATIVE in their play.

It is when the tables are set out and the children are buzzing that the teacher's work really begins.

It is now that the teacher's skills come into action

Stand back and examine what they are really doing. "Being busy" is not always enough. "Being busy" can often mean not thinking!!

Little Liza is poking clay and chasing round in a duck mask. She has also swirled purple paint on paper.

QUESTIONS

a) Is she doing this because the poor child has never met clay or paint, worn a duck mask and chased a boy? i.e. it is wonderful new experience.

b) Is she bored with poking clay and slopping paint? She has done it for two weeks or more. Mucking around with a boy and a duck mask is a fairly interesting time filler.

c) Is the boy she is chatting to a policeman? Is she a girl who has changed into a duck and is the clay her baby? And when...

The skilled teacher swiftly ascertains what Liza is really up to and either leaves her **or** *adds a bit of stimuli i.e. who looks after the baby now, you or the duck?* **or** *steps into the situation of boredom and revitalises it,* **or** *introduces a better activity.*

ARE THEY REALLY ???
Quiet and busy isn't always the answer ...

USEFUL QUOTES WHEN EXPLAINING THINGS TO PEOPLE WHO DON'T UNDERSTAND...

Not true 😊*

QUOTE FROM A LONGER ARTICLE WRITTEN BY THE OFSTED CHIEF INSPECTOR 2003

Just before Christmas, the parents of a seven-year-old asked whether the sterile nature of the education he was receiving was the inevitable consequence of government prescription. They described their son working through 'endless photocopied work-sheets in every subject', learning to spell lists of words before writing sentences to include them and being prevented from writing a story until he had learned the techniques of how to construct one.

John Clare was right when he replied that such sterility was the product of a poorly run school. Teaching of this kind would certainly be condemned by any Ofsted inspector. More importantly it would be very unlikely to result in high standards in English – or anything else for that matter – and it would certainly extinguish the natural enthusiasm for learning that most seven-year-olds possess in abundance.

He thought of the present world no longer as a wonderland of experiences, but as geography and history, as the repeating of names that were hard to pronounce, and lists of products and populations and heights and lengths and as lists and dates –

– oh! and Boredom indescribable.

He was uncertain about the spelling and pronunciation of most words in our beautiful and perplexing tongue ... that particularly was a pity because words attracted him and under happier conditions he might have used them well –

He was always doubtful whether it was eight sevens or nine eights that was sixty three (he knew of no way of settling the difficulty), and he thought the merit of drawing consisted in the care with which it was 'lined in'. Lining in bored him beyond measure.

Outside the regions devastated by the school curriculum he was still intensely curious.

Mr. Polly H.G. Wells

For a reason that takes too long to explain, the children in my class once told me that they had chosen "the best person in the class". I couldn't resist asking WHO and WHY. They declared unanimously that it was Annie. I was amazed. Todays inspectors would be stunned, for Annie was by S.A.T.S. standards a complete and utter failure.

Out of the mouths of babes and suckling . . .

ANNIE

circa 1970

Annie was super at telly
and knew every programme there was.
She was super at helping to tidy
  and cleaning
  and finding
  and jobs.
She was bestest at guessing and laughing,
at sorting – and putting away.
And sharing her crisps
and her peanuts,
inventing new games we could play.
She was smashing at jokes and at acting,
unknotting laces
and games.
She knew every face in the Infants
and called everyone by their names,
Penny
  Peter
    Paul
      and James...
Annie shared in all their games.
She always gave way in a squabble,
at teasing she never got wild –
but TESTERS said Annie was useless
and called her –
  A Less Able Child.

Pity poor Annie in 2004

I AM ACUTELY AWARE...

I am acutely aware of the fact that many readers will say:

FINE!
We see what you are getting at. We see what you mean.

Hopefully most will say:

We knew all this before, but it has given us a new confidence to develop creative and child-centred work in spite of Ofsted shackles and their dreadful mind numbing obsession with paperwork and with everything being planned to death.

BUT WHERE ARE THE EXAMPLES OF WHAT WE CAN DO TOMORROW?

Sorry!
There are not many in this book. It isn't that sort of publication.

In 1985 I published *Standpoint* and *Puddlejumping*.
These books were solid with practical ideas and sold in thousands.
At the outset of Ofsted and the National Curriculum sales zeroed. Perhaps I should reprint?
Do let me know!

By means of a suitable conclusion let us examine the two ways of teaching highlighted in this publication.

● A) THE SUBJECT APPROACH

● B) THE CHILD-CENTRED APPROACH

Example: Let us pretend that for some reason or other we want our children to learn about the weather. It could be anything: reading and maths to Romans or bullying, but today it is the weather.

The Weather...

A) The subject, fact-based, being told method (often sitting on the mat listening)

Probably the school will have a forward plan explaining how it is to be done (ugh!). **Plans, aims, targets, objectives, evaluations, tests, measurements and worksheets or exercise books, i.e. proof that targets have been hit.**

OK, videos, computers, even a trip outside to see the clouds, might feature, but it will inevitably be a fact and knowledge-based, skills focused lesson.

Not unlike the ones most of us experienced in secondary school science or geography for 45 mins, years ago.

B) The child-centred or 'brain neurons' approach

Sadly neurologists tell us children do not learn i.e. **retain and understand** information by merely being told. Or writing things down. Even if they can repeat information, it is not the way in which they form real concepts of understanding.

So we don't begin with the facts, we begin with finding the meaningful context.

At this particular moment in the writing of this booklet one of those magical moments of teaching arrived.

A reception class teacher - sorry, I don't know who... (but someone please tell me!) sent me the next two pages.

Following my talk somewhere she had a go.

Surely they are the best two pages of this publication. An inspiration to us all.

THANKS

Puddles!

Aims: to provide problem solving opportunities
Class of 20 children (5 Resource Base), one adult.

Children were asked to get into groups of four. This proved to be quite a challenge for the children and took some time.

We then went out into the Nursery playground in our groups and looked for signs of rain.
"It's on the floor"
"it's stopped raining in the sky now, cuz we come out"

The children were asked to go on a puddle hunt and find one special puddle.
Again this took a little time for some of the children to make their choice and agree on one puddle.

The children were asked to name their puddle. The children were told 'The puddle can only have one name so you must all think of names and then look at your puddle and agree on one name.' This again took some time. There was a lot of discussion. (It was interesting to observe that it was the 'more able' children who found this difficult.) I visited each group and asked them to introduce me to their puddles. The puddles were called Banana man, Fluffy, Noddy, Cabbage and Diamond-star. (The last one I was assured was one name.)

The children were then asked to draw around their puddle with chalk. One person was to draw round the puddle, while others were to check that they had not gone through the puddle or too far away from their puddle. This again provided a lot of discussion. The more dominant child in the group got to the chalk first, but the quieter child then became the one giving the instructions,
"He's all over here, you've gone in him"

The children were then asked to go and look at each others puddles, being careful not to step on Noddy, Cabbage, Fluffy or Diamond-star. They took great care and discussed size, and whether it was muddy or not.

The children were then instructed that I would like them to measure all the way around their puddle. They could use anything they wanted from the classroom.

This again took some time. All the children still came and asked if they could use equipment. The only answer I would give was, 'if you would like to, go and fetch it from the classroom'

I became more involved with one group who had three Resource Base children in it, asking simple questions to encourage descriptive words. With this group I found a piece of wool in my pocket and asked them if we could use this.

They took care when they put the wool around the edge, two other children correcting any errors in a very sensitive way. They found that the wool was too long, so they were asked how we could make it just right. They thought of scissors.

Other groups had used rulers (overlapping)
Lego bricks
Multi-link cubes
Unifix cubes

I asked them then to look at each other's puddles. Then we were going to take our measures into the classroom. This provided an opportunity for the Resource Base children to tell the others how they had used the wool. There was a lot of discussion and the other groups said they couldn't carry their measurements in and wanted to use wool. They were all given different coloured wool and given the instruction that they had to be careful and make sure they went all the way around their puddle.

One group of 'more able' boys took great care and cut the wool into little pieces all putting their piece next to the last persons. (I commented on how they had worked together and taken care).

The class was then asked to bring their measurements back into the class. We were going to hang them on the door to see how long they were. We started putting them up when the 'Banana man' group said
"Oh, we can't they're in little bits"

They were asked how they could make it into one long piece and they thought of sellotape straight away. They started taping the pieces together, but after about five minutes asked if they could have another piece of wool to do it again. The group had found that some of the wool would not stick because it was wet.

I was really impressed because they had seen the results of all the other groups hanging from the door and when they came back in they had 'manipulated' their results making sure their puddle measurement was the longest!

We went out at different times during the day to look at our puddles. The Diamond-star group asked if they could do theirs again because it had got smaller.

In the afternoon most of our puddles had gone. I asked where they had gone and they children came up with some lovely answers.

"It's dead"

"It's gone into the sky"

"It's gone down into the ground"

"The sun's come out, it's warm now and it's gone up into the sky"

This was one of those 'YES' moments you get and one I'll not forget.

The discussions, the children's enthusiasm and enjoyment and weather all went better than I could have imagined.

Children have since gone back to look for their puddles both during and after rain.

● Girls are doctors, boys are nurses and we 'examine' our own puddle.

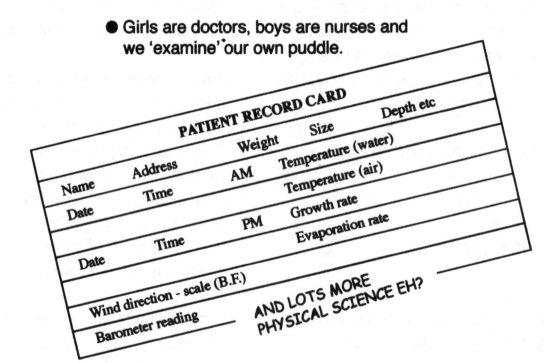

PATIENT RECORD CARD

Name	Address		Weight	Size	Depth etc
Date	Time	AM	Temperature (water)	
			Temperature (air)	
Date	Time	PM	Growth rate	
			Evaporation rate	
Wind direction - scale (B.F.)				
Barometer reading		AND LOTS MORE PHYSICAL SCIENCE EH?		

LOTS OF EXCITEMENT

Harry weighs 200gms

We've made
Jo red

We're going to wash
Jane in Teacher's
filter

Janet is
almost half a
litre

**AND NOW WE ARE GOING TO POUR THEM BACK AND
SEE THEM STOP AT THE MARK WE CHALKED ROUND**

TWO HOURS LATER

Harry has nearly
gone

Jo's gone! But the
red's here

Janet's shrunk away

Jane's nearly
gone

WHEN WILL THEY COME BACK?

Where have they gone?
Will it rain tomorrow?
When will it rain again, Miss?
I want Harry to return...

Success!

**They're eager. They're keen.
They want to be taught.**

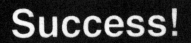

What on earth has been going on at school this week? When they get home they go on about their puddle or something...

THERE ARE ALL SORTS OF WAYS WE CAN FIND THAT OUT ABOUT HARRY

Let's go and look at the clouds...

Let's go and feel the wind...

Let's go and look at a little machine called a barometer...

Let's go and look at a weather map on TV...

Let me explain what you **WANT TO KNOW** and I will tell you, help you and **occasionally even test you!**

THIS, DEAR READER, IS REAL EDUCATION

Ofsted and the National Literacy Strategy are encouraging imagination in the classroom, not stifling it.

(David Bell, Head of Ofsted)

David seems a good chap and he was a primary schoolteacher! So why don't we test him out and put more imagination into the way in which we interpret those turgid Ofsted publications? I see they even have a new one called *Strategy for Enjoyment*. How ridiculous can we get? I believe it occurs in the third Thursday of each month beginning with a J.

Next time you have a planning meeting **BE BOLD... BE STRONG..** do a bit of puddlejumping. Why can't a fresh flowering of child centred learning begin in your classroom? OK, many teachers are too scared to step out of line. A union's recent attempt to get rid of S.A.T.S. was defeated... Believe it or not teachers voted to keep them!

We need to be courageous as we reinterpret dull documents – and creative as we replace them with work of genuine meaning and relevance to the children we have taken into our care.

Keep trying for the children's sake.

Peter Dixon
New Years Day 2004

P.S. I hope these wise words from John Clare in his *Daily Telegraph* Column will highlight the breadth of concern about Early Years Education:

> *One does not have to dispute that to wonder why the nursery sector has not risen up in rebellion. Or do teachers, who complain so bitterly about ticking boxes, find comfort in being told precisely what to do? Do they – or we – not mind that the Government is turning them into automata?*

CONCLUSION....

Readers might feel that I have overstated my case.

If it is overstated it is in direct response to the blitz of an attack made by Ofsted upon our schools and teachers.

Ofsted is relentless and anyone with even half a step in the world of primary schooling will know of teachers being stressed to the point of weariness and tears – even sometimes beyond – by the ridiculous demands being placed upon them.

Pointless demands – utterly divorced from the genuine needs of their children.

Foolish demands – often made by those who seek statistics to gain political or personal advantage.

I have, however, a positive conclusion and it comes from David Bell (2003) HMI Inspector of Schools.

TEACHERS HAVE TO REGAIN THE INITIATIVE AND NOT REGARD THEMSELVES AS HELPLESS VICTIMS OF INSTRUCTIONS FROM ABOVE

Rejoice my friends! The Chief Inspector tells us to regain the initiative. Pin this message to the staff-room door. Read it every morning. Read it at every staff meeting. We are not helpless victims...

It is up to us to develop the exciting patterns of work which are our children's rights to enjoy.

And if the Chief Inspector of Schools is for us, then who can be against us!

THE RIVERSIDE NURSERY SCHOOL

Winchester City Football Club, Hillier Way, Abbots Barton, Winchester SO23 7SU

7 February 2005

Dear Parents

During next term we will be encouraging the children to undertake a project based on a topic of their own choice. We will begin by talking and listening to the children to find out what interests them.

We want the children to have a large input into how the project develops and we will keep a visual record of what they do using annotated photographs. It is possible the project maybe exhausted in one week or it may go on for the whole half-term with the children revisiting ideas.

The project may begin outdoors in the home corner or with a large craft or paint and clay activity, that may subsequently trigger new ideas for the children. The outcome will not be predetermined, but will develop as the term moves along.

Of course the other activities at nursery will continue as normal such as art and craft, puzzles, construction toys, role play and our outdoor activities.

You can help your child to contribute by encouraging them to tell us about anything exciting they have enjoyed over the half-term holiday or of anything that has captured their imagination.

We would welcome contributions by way of 'junk' for modelling and particularly any natural resources we can use that you might find when out and about in the woods, at the beach or from your garden.

We hope this will be fun for the children and encourage them to feel more involved in nursery topics. If you have any questions please don't hesitate to ask.

Half-term is next week and we return on 21st February

Hope you all have a super half-term.

Best regards

Beverly Feeney

A JUNIOR SCHOOL

Dear Parents

30th September 1988

In our work so far this term we have been thinking about our families and our school. Now we are going outwards into the community and during the next two weeks we are thinking about Doctors, Nurses, Ambulancemen and Hospital workers. In order to start off the topic with some drama, I have asked the children if they could come on Monday morning with an imaginary wound bandaged up! I know Monday mornings are a bit fraught but I would be grateful if you could help. Don't worry about proper bandaging – an old sheet or towel or something would do – but please do it up firmly so that it will stay on for a couple of hours.

Thank you very much.

With very best wishes

Mary Lock

If some schools are brave enough to stand by their beliefs... then why not more?

BETWEEN 3 YEARS AND 5 YEARS OUR CHILDREN HAVE 3 SUMMERS. THAT'S ALL ... HOW ARE THEY GOING TO SPEND THEM?

IT IS UP TO US.

Minimal planning!
Bursting with pride!

Neither of these phrases are very often associated with staffroom chat. All too often such conversation focuses gloomily upon the struggle of the paper work and new government directives.

SO...

I hope this letter will act as a suitable finalé. Something to encourage you, as much as myself.

Dear Peter,

I don't know if you remember me but you visited our school in Clevedon last year to deliver a wonderful in-service day. I have written to you since then and was delighted when you wrote back to me. I have been meaning to reply ever since but time has gone on......

You asked me in your last letter if things were really changing in early education- and I truly think that change is beginning. As I said in my original letter to you, you really changed the way that I approach my teaching. I was so inspired when I heard you talk at an Early Years Conference in Weston Super Mare and I have continued to use your books and poetry as sources of inspiration to me and as tools to inspire and challenge others. I often quote your poetry at our Parents Induction Meeting when I inform them that we "Jump Puddles" (as well as naming them and collecting them in jars) and that no child will leave our Foundation Stage Classrooms clutching "Silver Toilet Roll Holders" or anything that resembles adult influenced, mass produced and therefore pointless "craft".

The last couple of years have been wonderfully liberating although the first parents evening was a little scary. I had virtually nothing to show the parents as everything the children had made, written, created etc they had proudly taken home on the day of creation. I found that I didn't need to show the parents anything "concrete" because I could talk about each individual child at length and with great personal detail. I didn't need to talk blandly about phonic knowledge and number symbol recognition because I could talk about the actual children, citing whole episodes of their play that illustrated their learning. I knew their children's passions, their preferred learning styles, their language patterns, what made them laugh and what they hated doing and avoided at all costs! I also knew that they all rushed into school (often round the back before I had "officially" opened the doors!) because they loved coming and I was so proud that I felt I could burst. You said that children will follow you wherever you take them -take them to good places, and I truly try to do this every day-and it's fab. My planning is minimal and I find it difficult to explain to my many visitors exactly how I run the classroom -because I don't- the children do - and it works!!! I do document what the children do and I use photographs to show the processes that they go through in all areas of their learning but I'm never really sure what tomorrow will bring!

This attitude is spreading amongst colleagues both in and out of my school. I recently started a local, informal cluster group with a like-minded colleague and I now work in pre-schools for a day a week - constantly giving the same message about the way we should be working with children. I recently gave a talk to new parents at a pre-school and used your work again to illustrate point. I also listened to Ros Bayley at an Early Years Conference in April and she read out "We're Going on a Bear Hunt" as part of her wonderful dialogue. I'm aware that this letter is a bit of a stream of consciousness but I will always be so grateful to you for your assistance on my journey, and I know that your work and your beliefs help to inspire people to CHANGE - which is wonderful.

Anyway I'm sure you are very busy and will be very grateful if you have taken time to read this. I hope that this will hearten you and will help in some small way in your crusade to change education.

GAIL ALDER

ODE TO AUTUMN

Today we will read a beautiful poem.
It is a literacy hour poem
so we will only read half.
First we will count the adjectives,
afterwards the nouns.

Dear Parent

The success of your child's day at school does not really depend upon them being 'kept busy' or 'quiet'. Or even in the production of something to take home.

It's so much more than that. Teaching is not that simple!

As has already been explained, children do not learn by merely being told. They need to learn in a meaningful context and in an enjoyable way... usually associated with the process of play.

So....

The person who teaches your child has to work very hard to make, invent, design, prepare and organise these purposeful learning activities. Added to this, they have to think clearly about YOUR CHILD as an individual. And everyone else's child too! *What is their individual need? What is their stage of development, particular requirement, both as a youngster in their own right and also as a group or whole class member. In what area will they need extra help, reinforcement or perhaps increased demands to be made?*

It is very hard to plan for all these things, but that is what skilful, child-focused teachers try to do. It's their job.

They might be lousy cooks or accountants, but their training will have enabled them to PLAN for days which will stimulate, enrich and delight your child.

IT IS CALLED CHILD-CENTRED TEACHING.

It is a style of teaching founded upon childhood itself.

Teachers who work in this way have a tough time. Quite often Headteachers are fearful of straying away from narrow National Curriculum directives and inspectors are rarely understanding.

Children need to enjoy school ... to LOVE going ... homework should be needless.

Please support those teachers who, in increasing numbers, are seeking to allow children to be CHILDREN. It must be done.

AH-BUT PRIMARY

Ah but it's the parents,
    the children,
    the head,
    the governors,
    the Ofsted,
    the things that were said.

Ah but it's the storage
the money, the floors,
the cleaners, the helpers
the safety, the doors.

Ah but it's the targets,
assessments and SATS,
management, teachers,
uniforms, hats...

Our children are different,
our children can't sit.
They wriggle, they chatter,
our children have nits...

Our problems are awful –
we'd love you to call,
but we haven't the parking
and our staffrooms too small.

Peter Dixon

Contact Address:
30 Cheriton Road
Winchester
Hampshire SO22 5AX
Tel. 01962 854607

I DIDN'T LIKE READING AND WRITING when I was at school. I couldn't spell, understand adverbs or do comprehension exercises properly. I did write at home (secretly) but never showed people what had written in case they said it was all wrong.

I can't remember my mum or dad reading to me very much either and I don't think I ever really wanted them to... Anyway my dad was away fighting Hitler and he was in a prisoner of war camp. (He wasn't really but I always told people he was).

I do remember my lovely mum, however. She was a brilliant mother and often used to take her false teeth out and chase us around the house pretending to be a witch. It seemed better than being read to.

I loved going out to play and boxing much more than books – although *The Beano* and *The Hotspur* were OK. The clever kids read 'sensible' comics like *The Eagle* but I didn't.

Wife? Just the one and children (one of each kind). House? Yes, with posh front gates and a pond!

Before becoming a full-time writer I was a senior lecturer in education. I don't quite know how I got a smart job like that. I just did.

Selected Titles

Grow your own Poems
(Peche Luna)

The Colour of my Dreams
(Macmillan Children's Books)

Peter Dixon's Poetry Grand Prix
(Macmillan Children's Books)

Penguin in the Fridge
(Macmillan Children's Books)

Juggler (Barrington Stoke)

Favourite book: Just William by Richmal Crompton

Favourite food: Crackle on pork

Favourite word: Macmillan

Favourite place: Whitby where I spent lots of my childhood getting wet.

Where do your ideas come from?
Rusty tins and funny faces,
pretty gardens, ugly places.
Dogs and cats and kangaroos,
people's socks and people's shoes
Tears and sadness – people starving
Killing sharks (DON'T)... and well, just about anything other than spring, bonfire night and windy days. I don't write about things that there are already hundreds of poems about.

What else might you have been?
If it wasn't wicked and bad and wrong and awful, I'd have been a burglar. It must be fun creeping about in dark houses - sorting through things. But I can't. And neither can you! So I suppose my second thing would be either a Harrier pilot or a beachcomber.

Text from: *The Children's Authors Address Book*, Gervase Phinn, LDA
ISBN 1 85503 3550.

Extract

Roger's Daddy's clever
Daisy's flies a plane
Michael's does computers
and has a house in Spain.
Lucy's goes to London,
he stays there every week ...
    But my Daddy has an ear-ring
      and lovely dancing feet.
He hasn't got a brief case,
he hasn't got a phone
he hasn't got mortgage
and we haven't got a home.
He hasn't got a fax machine
we haven't got a car.
    But he can dance and fiddle
    and my Daddy is
    a Star.

From
Peter Dixon's Poetry Grand Prix
(Macmillan Children's Books)

CONFERENCES
SCHOOLS
Surprising though it may seem...

PETER DIXON (sometime school teacher and eventually senior lecturer in education) is a much sought after conference and after dinner speaker.

Also with humorist, songwriter and guitarist Mr Geoffrey Ridden, a cabaret artist capable of entertaining audiences willing to enjoy the lampooning of such sacred names as Paul McCartney and even the 'Lady in Red' man.

Peter and Geoff's travels have included 'Parents' Evenings' in Basingstoke, Officers' Messes in Rheindahlen and the Edinburgh Festival (Pete) and New Faces TV (Geoff).

So whether it's verse, song and wine or the education key note speaker you require...

Phone 01962 854607

Geoff Ridden and Peter Dixon

An incomparable evening of poetry, music and relevant irreverence! Between them, Pete and Geoff have over one hundred years experience of entertaining, badgering and pummelling audiences into submission. Pete has recently toured Belgium with Benjamin Zephaniah and last November could be found tired and emotional on a Cypriot beach with Forkbeard Fantasy. Geoff is a man who needs no introduction ... at least not to his wife and the local constabulary. A man whose beard goes before him and whose trousers follow shortly after ... a guitarist of immeasurable talent and height. The Flanders and Swann of the new millennium, the Eric and Ernie of post-modern vaudeville. A must for the special conference or school evening.

PECHE LUNA BOOKS

If you have enjoyed – wept or sighed, laughed or smiled at any poems in this 'oh so serious' booklet...

Why not treat yourself to a copy of *Weepers*, a collection of poems about schools (and you know who) guaranteed to raise the spirit of the weariest staffroom.